Motive and
Opportunity

Also by the author

Imperfect Music (Modena: Edizioni Galleria Mazzoli, 2019)
Toodle-oo (Los Angeles / Bagnone: Magra Books, 2017)
Border Music (Greenfield, MA: Talisman House, 2016)
Solitude (Modena: Edizioni Mazzoli, 2015)
Six White Mules / Sei muli bianchi (Milano: Edizioni del Verri, 2014)
Wholly Falsetto with People Dancing (Los Angeles: Seismicity Eds, 2013)
Mapping Stone (with Dennis Phillips, Milano / Los Angeles: postmedia
    books / Seismicity Editions, 2013)
Two (Greenfield, MA: Talisman House, 2010)
Azusa: a Sequel (Los Angeles: Pie In The Sky Press, 2009)
La vita semplice / A Simple Life (Modena: Galleria Mazzoli, 2009)
Alphabet 2007 / Alfabeto 2007 (Modena: Galleria Mazzoli, 2007)
Days Shadows Pass (Los Angeles: Green Integer, 2006)
Caper (2 vols., with Ray DiPalma, Piacenza: ML & NLF, 2006)
Agency (Los Angeles: Seeing Eye Books, 2003)
Embarrassment of Survival: Selected Poems, 1970-2000 (New York:
    Marsilio / Agincourt Editions, 2001)
Alphabets (Los Angeles: Littoral Books, 1999)
A Life (Piacenza: ML&NLF, 1997)
Luci e colori d'Italia (Mantova: Corradini Editore, 1996)
Nemo (Los Angeles: Sun & Moon Books, 1995)
The Simple Life (Modena: Lab. d'Arte Grafica Roberto Gatti, 1993)
Villa (Littoral Books, 1991)
Domain (with G.T. James and Joe Goode; Los Angeles & San Francisco:
    Red Hill Press / Invisible City Editions, 1986)
Rime (Red Hill Press, 1983)
Abandoned Latitudes: Three Los Angeles Writers (with Robert Crosson &
    John Thomas; Red Hill Press, 1983)
Another You (Red Hill, 1981)
Un grammo d'oro (Rome: Cervo Volante, 1981)
Portfolio (Los Angeles & Fairfax, CA: Red Hill, 1978)
Remembering the Movies (Red Hill, 1977)
2 x 2 (Red Hill, 1977)
La stanza stravagante (Turin: Edizioni Geiger, 1976)
The Extravagant Room (Red Hill Press, 1976)
Pearl Harbor (San Francisco: Isthmus Press, 1975)
Il tenero continente (Turin: Edizioni Geiger, 1975)
The Tender Continent (Los Angeles: Chatterton's Bookstore, 1974)
Air (Red Hill Press, 1973)
Communion (Fairfax, CA: Red Hill, 1970)

Paul Vangelisti

MOTIVE AND OPPORTUNITY

Shearsman Books

First published in the United Kingdom in 2020 by
Shearsman Books Ltd
PO Box 4239
Swindon
SN3 9FN

Shearsman Books Ltd Registered Office
30–31 St. James Place, Mangotsfield, Bristol BS16 9JB
(this address not for correspondence)

www.shearsman.com

ISBN 978-1-84861-715-5

CONTENTS

DRIVING PLATITUDES

for Dennis Phillips

"A rather open scrawl while one's eyes are fixed on the road
is the only trick to be mastered."
—Ed Dorn, *Hello, La Jolla*

1.

A sliver of a moon given way to gibbous.
The blue hour leaves dusk with a tinge of ending.

And, of course, a labyrinth with a bad boy
at its center and the ungodly habit

of consuming uninvited and invited guests.
What in the puzzle relishing a traveler's flesh,

what half – queen or anointed bull – enforces
this contorted way to offending knowledge?

2.

And not *labrum* but *librum*, 'from the bark
of a tree,' a melody certainly other.

Poetry now an eccentricity to what
accompanies the maintenance of empire.

And the *mot juste*, the clarity that
people were censored, exiled, imprisoned,

flayed alive even and dismembered for.
And the cosmos, Dennis, streaming west

on Beverly behind the windshield.

3.

And in this world a furled shadow
sublime, beckoning in obscurity.

There's no message. The message is that
love too would eat the red wheelbarrow.

A membrane of text between us, scant,
irreparable maybe, with your name on it.

4.

Potentiality: that bald soprano of our immigrant
upbringing. *Our* – in the sense of continuity,

sisters and brothers of willing catastrophe.
Strictly from hunger, in those raw collages

of the streets. Unrelenting we've become
for the right word, or just plain lost

in the anagrams of such desiring?

5.

A difficult harmony to build a song on
sung in a decidedly minor key.

Does a minotaur rise like an ill-translated miner
from the dankest earth? Does he too dream

of wealth buried deep within a body?

6.

Our lesser half rises early enough
with morning light to dispel the nightly dread.

A kind of fussiness – *spell, dispel* –
bracketing the story of how
that Depression-era Mouse
perched on Disney's shoulder
in the margin of a dictionary.

7.

We were expecting rain and instead –
O small wind, O tepid light –

a mostly pleasurable afternoon,
cloud and lingering smog on the horizon.

The 'will to change' (Olson's words)
less willful, more mechanical daily.

Depending on the lives of those who risk
living in that quiet way. Curious,

my beauties, the angels we're becoming.

8.

Now after the rain our city shines
like no other with the hope of beginning.
Here spring has sprung no matter what time of year
and breezy overture to an always

unfinished melodrama. May we too shine
as March in this illustrious wind.

9.

Even with everything east on Beverly, west
on Beverly, despite a drought at the heart

of singing. The air heavy with harmonies
of sex, spring tides on heavy sand,

woodpecker's rat-tat-tat, hawk's wheeling plaint
above the arroyo. Here we are *home again,*

home again, jigeddy-jig, as Bob liked to say,
every time we crested the hill and rolled down

the other side of Cerro Gordo.

10.

Come, traveler, lay back in your armchair
with the faintest of melodies and

missing words. Cradle the book
on your left, puzzling the rise and fall

and who may hear simple phrases
and sometimes facts lingering in the tweak

of a dusky breeze on the hillside.
The moon returns underwater

rising to you in greeny choruses,
bubbly labyrinth, a boy at its core.

THE GRID

for George Fekaris

"Very much a place that refuses to know itself."
Carey McWilliams, *Southern California Country*

1.

Unending summer's idyll
with breeze seeping easterly.
Avenues and empty streets
enlisted, north to south,
east to west. Who can deny
that tiny older gent
flourishing Tai-chi
in 90 degree heat
at a bus stop? Lying
as one must, words turn up
like assassins in love
in a near faultless grid
across the city.

2.

The girl's as good an excuse
as any. Air follows light
in the logic of August
and pretext spells *dodge*,
a once-upon-a-time word
few would ever think
of tuning. The grid's funny
as it gets, meandering
through a drunken forest.
"Hold the onions, please,"
exclaims the jealous widow.
Some days, he thinks, some days.
Butterflies don't tell much
all things to the contrary.
Habits are simply habits,
sleep rounder than the moon.
The girl and the grid.
Rounder. Habits. Please.

3.

Beware the ever constant moon,
and the first thing coming
like the Mojave Desert
or the appalling name
Red Rock Canyon. A New
World coinage for valleys
of different sizes. And an
even smaller *arroyo*
from where I speak.
In this wayward basin
it's mostly emblems
and another name
for the previous girl.

4.

The island's visible
only to aspiring,
and confidence spells
money in the bank.
At stale summer's end,
most brutal of seasons,
skill and technique repeat
the drunken forest.
Out here the con's always on:
with jaded syncopation
and a tattered back-beat.
 Stale. Summer. Drunken skill.
Sometimes one can hear
the whistle a-blowing.
Had there not been a child
or the end of the war.

5.

A towhee, one supposes,
melozone crissalis,
knows the morning well –
bath, briefest song and
a thin parting *tseeee.*
One's confident of
the towhee, chancing
the sluggish burbling
of a fountain, the hillside
barrenness. The name calls
like Red Rock Canyon
or the missing girl. Towhee.

6.

And the straggly palm
glimmering on the hill
above the car wash.
Hardly the end of the mind.
Paper moon, cardboard sky.
But an end nonetheless,
if not a purpose –
a conviction, rather,
reducing the mind to
 gathering information.
Pragmatism. *Thing-ism.*
The cacti croon night and day
about the end of time
and what could've been.
Sincerity's everything
south of parody.

7.

Or poverty. Desert flowers
and such expensive hips.
Hard-boiled, one might add,
not taking into account
the fire that rings her eyes
and the scant melody.
The recipe, of course,
given silly sex or
even sillier dying.
Linger here awhile
 before the stale night
and a westerly breeze
now entirely missing.
Like our assassin
most deeply in love,
shot clean through the heart
sitting on the crapper.

8.

Is it stone that's moral
or the song? The birds
have just about finished
as the morning heats
and the light swells each
corner of the garden.
Nature, we are taught,
maintains amoral,
like the scrub jay on the porch
weighing what ought to be
most apt of the four
peanuts on the railing.
Does or *must* he pick,
and why a lusty shriek
to announce each choosing?
Soon no sound but a gurgling
fountain and the occasional
truck wheezing uphill.

9.

Is it truly suffering
or the shame of suffering
that endures? To catch fire
in a word or two.
La musica imperfetta.
Who waits in the garden,
there, not there, a shadow
beyond the porch. The question
is the question, gusting
welcome or unwelcome
from the other side of
the desert. Here, not here,
a far older melody.

10.

Poetry anticipates thought
as, of course, technique
and the wind in love.
As our dead turn up
whispering at a bus stop,
and their delicate sense.
Traffic's not a question or
likely name for a sequel.
As we know little of
composer Franceschini's
birth (1730-
something), and equally
little of his death
(1790-something).
The logic of August
following butterflies
through the jealous forest.

11.

Fire in the garden
rounder than the moon,
 a corner in shadow.
Is it song carries one
so far or the singing?
Is it time one walks in
or is it space convening
at nightfall dances here?
Is it a melody
or stone one fixes
so early of a morning,
repeating the order
of thought, of steps taken
to a dim waking? Fire.
Night song. Dancing this far.

LOUIS IX RECALLING HIS CRUSADES

for Michael C. McMillen

Harry Truman, we are told, liked to get up early and walk over to the National Gallery. With much of the city still asleep, the President would nod silently to the guard whose special duty it was to open up for him. Here, what passes for urbanity holds that we live in such an illusory and unintelligible place – and we like it. Antechamber, if not final destination, as native son Charles Bukowski liked to say, "for all the assholes in the world and mine." It was a reasonably shabby door at the end of a reasonably shabby corridor in the sort of building that was new about the year the all-tile bathroom became the basis of civilization.

Truman savored his visits to the Old Masters and recorded them in his diary, observing on one occasion, "It's a pleasure to look at perfection and then think of the lazy, nutty moderns. It is like comparing Christ with Lenin." An old woman peddles crack in a driveway on Pico, just east of Crenshaw, and before long the writer will reach home and get down to cooking dinner. "A curve, a slider, a duck bounced foul to the right side," announces the car radio, a warm late October afternoon and what more to long for?

Truman articulated a view held by many Americans when we were boys, linking experimental art to degenerate or subversive impulses, with this attitude culminating in attacks on the floor of Congress: "Ultramodern artists are unconsciously being used as tools of the Kremlin." Solo or somehow optimistic as to the love that upholds the planets and the cold in one's bones. Down by any old second-hand sea, where the prairie flows in nameless light.

But if the President, politicians and the general public saw in the new art signs of Communist subversion, America's cultural mandarins found a contrary virtue: for them the new art, and the New York School's Abstract Expressionism in particular, spoke to a specifically anti-Communist ideology. "Free enterprise painting" is what Nelson Rockefeller was fond of calling it. [A DOWNTOWN INTERSECTION in Los Angeles fades in: It is night, about two o'clock, very little traffic.] This was more than thirty years before Nelson, as Vice-President of the United States, gave the finger to a crowd of students at the State University of New

York at Binghamton, September 17, 1976. The "Rockefinger" or "Rockefeller salute," as some pundits came to call it, would take its place as a fitting adornment to our Bicentennial celebration. [At the left and in the immediate foreground a traffic signal stands at GO.]

Non-figurative and politically silent, the antithesis of socialist realism, it was a clearly American intervention. Meow, insisted the feline, demure in her basic black. No way to make a living or a life, replied the stairway used in case of fire. As early as 1946, critics were applauding the new art as 'independent, self-reliant, a true expression of the national will, spirit and character.' Hardly matters that before long it would end up being push 'em up, Tony, and poodles at the Ritz. The new painting was seen to uphold the Yankee myth of the lone voice, the intrepid individual, a tradition Hollywood mined in films such as *Mr. Smith Goes to Washington* and *Twelve Angry Men*. Contrary to how just about anybody watches his or her language. As far as poetry speaks mostly to the dead.

Eventually to return to that one thing resounding like the scene of the crime. Willem de Kooning talked about a dream he'd once had of Pollock busting through the doors of a bar like a Hollywood cowboy, shouting, "I can paint better than anybody." A mild June evening, dusk unfurling across the boulevard just west of the San Diego Freeway, motorcycle revving its engine twice, like gunfire. By 1948, Clement Greenberg was making claims for the new, Cold War aesthetic: "The conclusion forces itself, much to our own surprise, that the main premises of Western Art have at last migrated to New York and the United States, along with the center of gravity of industrial production and political power."

I didn't know what time it was: piped-in Della Reese insisting against a hillside of bulldozed earth, clichés lining up like freshly painted parking slots in front of a new Starbucks. O.K., Captain, full speed ahead, my father liked to repeat from his wheelchair strapped into the center of a van on his way to the doctor's. Commenting on this claim, Jason Epstein would later say: "America – and especially New York – had now become the center of the world politically and financially and, of course, the center culturally too. Well, what would a great power be without an appropriate art? You couldn't be a great power if you didn't have the art to go with it."

The hills were still green and in the valley across the Hollywood Hills you could see snow on the high mountains. The notion that Abstract Expressionism could become a vehicle for the imperial burden was beginning to take hold. The fur stores were advertising their annual sales. The call houses that specialize in sixteen-year-old virgins were doing land-office business. And in Beverly Hills the jacaranda trees were almost in full bloom. But its emergence in those early years of the Cold War presented its promoters with a serious dilemma. "We had a lot of trouble with members of Congress," CIA agent and cultural czar Tom Braden later recalled. "They couldn't stand modern art. They thought it was a travesty, they thought it was sinful, they thought it was ugly." When we were boys.

Brahms Piano Quartet in F, op 34: an aesthetic fact, gloriously outlandish, east on Beverly, west on Beverly. "That's one of the reasons why it had to be done covertly," Braden added, "it had to be covert because it would have been turned down if it had been put to a vote. In order to encourage openness we had to be secret." Not the 'experience of experience,' a little too academic for my disposition, but/and experience in all its burning, savage, sweet complexity. Then her head went down and her right hand took the top card off the pack held in her left hand and turned it and her eyes looked at it and she added it to the pile of unplayed cards below the layout, and then turned the next card, quietly, calmly, in a hand steady as a stone pier in a light breeze. "What a world," said our angel in décolleté, "and so soon after what happened."

The Agency was aware that most New Yorkers came from somewhere sentimentally else, and it too looked for out-of-town help. Enough of the genuine – that was for hicks and tourists and everybody knew it. "Regarding abstract expressionism, I'd love to be able to say that the CIA invented it all, just to see what happened in New York and downtown SoHo tomorrow," joked Agency man Donald Jameson, before moving on to a more pragmatic explanation of CIA involvement.

"Of course, it could only have been done through the organizations or the operations of the CIA two or three removed," Agent Jameson went on, "so that there wouldn't have to be any question of having to clear Jackson Pollock, for example, or do anything that would involve these people in the organization— they'd just be cleared at the end of the line." East on Beverly and west, a solution as oblique as the crime. Jameson concluded, "If you had to use people who considered themselves one way or another closer to Moscow than to Washington, so much the better perhaps."

Once again, the CIA turned to the private sector to advance its objective, in this case the Museum of Modern Art in New York. A new moon hung above Sts. Peter & Paul and the blue neon hands on the Bonnier Building showed the time. Twenty minutes to two. MoMA's president through most of the 1940s and 1950s was Nelson Rockefeller, whose mother, Abby Aldrich Rockefeller, had co-founded the museum in 1929 (Nelson called it 'Mommy's Museum'). At that instant, the man sitting in the dark car was precisely thirty-six years old. His jaw was long and bony, his chin a jutting v under the more flexible v of his mouth. His nostrils curved back to make another, smaller v.

Nelson was an avid supporter of abstract expressionism with his private collection swelling to over 2,500 works, while thousands more covered the walls of buildings belonging to the Rockefeller family's Chase Manhattan Bank. The v motif was picked up again by thickish brows rising outward from twin creases above a hooked nose, and his pale brown hair grew down – from high flat temples – in a point on his forehead. When challenged over her decision to promote the Mexican revolutionary Diego Rivera, Abby Aldrich Rockefeller emphasized that the Reds would stop being Reds "if only we could get them artistic recognition." He stepped out into the night and slammed the car door behind him, looking rather pleasantly like a blond Satan.

The day was still only an hour and forty minutes old and nothing in particular had happened. Years before, in his infamous article in *Partisan Review*, "Avant-Garde and Kitsch," Greenberg spelled out the ideological rationale for seeking sponsorship from enlightened patrons, such as the Rockefellers and the CIA. Rarely does such a rime reach itself as the black cat licking just about under her tail. Greenberg's essay still stands as an article of faith for the anti-Marxist view of modernism, asserting that the avant-garde had been "abandoned by those to whom it actually belongs – our ruling class." The voice on the telephone seemed to be sharp and peremptory, but he didn't hear too well what it said – partly because he was only half awake and partly because he was holding the receiver upside down.

In the United States, as in the European past, "the umbilical cord of gold" must thrive, argued Greenberg, between the new art and the elite among the ruling classes. In fact, there was a man quite early this morning striding downhill in drizzling rain, a paper under his arm. First and foremost was Nelson Rockefeller himself, who had headed up the government's wartime intelligence agency for Latin America, named the Coordinator of Inter-American Affairs (CIAA). Among other activities, the agency sponsored touring exhibitions of 'contemporary American painting,' with nineteen of these shows subcontracted to MoMA. Long valleys are not so long that we cannot remember. Unless, of course, it's stopped raining and uneven birdsong has begun to outdo the dripping eaves.

The city woke up and yawned and stretched. As a trustee of the Rockefeller Brothers fund, a New York think-tank subcontracted by the government to study foreign affairs, Nelson presided over some of the most influential minds of the period as they established definitions of U.S. foreign policy. As did Agent

Larsson, woke up and yawned and stretched. In the early 1950s, Rockefeller was briefed on covert activities from Allen Dulles and Tom Braden, who later said, "I assumed Nelson knew pretty much everything about what we were doing." Exactly how much was the flower to linger in this extravagant room?

He put on his bathrobe and slippers and walked over to the window to check the weather. Rockefeller's close friend was John "Jock" Whitney, a long-time trustee of MoMA, who also served as its president and chairman of the board. As director of Rockefeller's motion picture division at CIAA in 1940-42, Jock oversaw production of such films as Disney's Saludas Amigos, brimming with goodwill toward our Latin neighbors. The wind was all gone but the air still had that dryness and lightness of the desert. As long as you recall how mountain and river sung before the malingering dust and leaves. After the war, he set up J.H. Whitney & Co., as "a partnership dedicated to the propagation of the free-enterprise system by the furnishing of financial backing for new, undeveloped, and risky businesses that might have trouble attracting investment capital through more conservative channels." O little star over the Amazon, says the impossible otter, how are you doing up there?

A prominent partner was William H. Jackson, a polo-playing friend of Jock's, who also happened to be deputy director of the CIA. This much faltering and how realism fifty years ago, just before the 2nd Street tunnel, a tatty dress and white socks and pumps skipping rope at dusk on an empty sidewalk. Another link was William Burden, who first joined the museum as chairman of its Advisory Committee in 1940, and also worked for Rockefeller's CIAA during the war. Then he looked into the mirror and saw a large bald man badly in need of a shave. Language, he thought, a perfect stranger or else. Chairing numerous quasi-governmental bodies, and even holding the presidency of the Farfield Foundation (the CIA's non-profit cultural conduit for gifts to such agencies as the Ford and Rockefeller Foundations), Burden was appointed chairman, in 1947, of the Committee on Museum Collections, and in 1956 he became MoMA's president. While showering he wondered if he would die that day.

It was not foreboding. He'd wondered the same thing every morning since he was eight years old and brushed his teeth before going off to school. William Paley, heir to the Congress Cigar Company, was yet another MoMA trustee with close ties to the Agency. A few miles past an act of kindness, or the optimism such lavish strangers leave on our Far Western landscape? A personal friend of Allen Dulles, Paley allowed his CBS network to provide cover for CIA operatives, an arrangement similar to that authorized by Henry Luce (also a MoMA trustee) at his *Time-Life* empire. About Paley's role with the CIA, one of his executives at CBS would years later recall, "It's the single subject about which his memory has failed."

There was just enough fog to make everything seem unreal. The time was three minutes past eleven on the evening of the thirteenth of November, 1967. On and on go the names, on and on go the connections. He checked the numerals on the clock, closed his eyes and fell asleep. Joseph Verner Reed, for instance, was a MoMA trustee at the same time he was a trustee for the Farfield Foundation, the CIA conduit. So was Gardner Cowles. So was Junkie Fleischman. So was Cass Canfield. And beyond those? The solemn cacti of Mexicali, the heartbreak of Buenos Aires?

The agents leaned over the table and studied the pictures of the unknown man. Oveta Culp Hobby, a founding member of MoMA, sat on the board of the Free Europe Committee, and allowed her family foundation in Texas to be used as yet another CIA conduit. The man had slithered down in the seat and lay sprawled against the back with his arms hanging and his left leg stuck out in the aisle. While she was Secretary of State for Health, Education and Welfare under Eisenhower, Hobby's assistant was one Joan Braden, who had previously worked for Nelson Rockefeller. Joan was married to Tom, the CIA agent who put together the International Organizations Division, nerve center of the clandestine cultural Cold War, which also ran dozens of fronts, including the Congress for Cultural Freedom, at the heart of the 1967 scandal with *Encounter* magazine. The front of the unknown man's coat was soaked with blood. He had no face left.

Regardless of the weather some are gifted with a sunny rump, contributing to a gradual lift in the atmospheric pressure, a rift in the gathering clouds and that ridiculous, if persistent notion that love is just around the corner. Before joining the CIA, Tom Braden had also worked for Rockefeller, as MoMA's executive secretary from 1947–1949. In Barcelona, a critic reviewing "The New American Painting," which MoMA toured that year, was appalled to learn that two canvases were so big that the upper part of the metal entrance door of the museum had to be sawn off to get them in. "You know one should never ask what one thinks," the Old Man was fond of reminding, "only what one knows or suspects. Keeping in mind, at times, a tiny, shriveled palm, at others, a giant ear of corn."

The white moonlight was cold and clear, like the justice we dream of but don't find. References to the size, the violence of the Wild West abounded, "as if the critics got hold of the wrong catalog, and thought the pictures were painted by Wyatt Earp or Billy the Kid," the Agency man recalled. It was already past midnight and there hadn't been a sound. Stop illustrating the goddamn passage, he thought, it's not that much further. A doctor entered the room.

The whispering became a mere sound. His fondness for moral positions in literature was lost watching the crimes of the Ford, Carter, Reagan and Bush Sr. administrations, and what managed to survive pillaged day after day during the reigns of Clinton and Bush Jr. The detective had just opened his mouth to repeat question number two when the unknown man in bed turned his head to the left.

Maybe Dwight Macdonald was right when he wrote: "Few Americans care to argue with a hundred million dollars." Or the narrator, in Saul Bellow's *Humboldt's Gift*, when he notes: "The country is proud of its dead poets. It takes terrific satisfaction in the poet's testimony that the USA is too tough, too big, too much, too rugged, that American reality is overpowering. So poets are loved, but loved because they just can't make it here."

The lower jaw slipped down and a slimy, blood-streaked pulp welled out of the unknown man's mouth. Where to begin? How to restore a history most aren't even aware is missing? A badly amplified, crackling blues echoed around the arroyo just after dark. Dogs howled. A car was whining up the hill.

With his back pinned alongside the doorway, he thought, who wants to say it? Especially now. Shadows grappled in something looking like a tango when he heard the shot.

Los Angeles,
April 2011

EYES CLOSED

for William Xerra

the last thing seen
as one would
sometimes in a dream
like a rose
in a guessing game
You go to my head

*

see the tower
see the steeple
leaving the night
to crowd this room
indefinitely

*

whisper of heels
on pavement
who never does
nor succumbs
to light

*

forming letters
falling and mounting
far short
of the page's
shallow mercy

*

no sound or word
for opening
eyes shut
nothing like ice cream
or any other scream
at the scene of a crime

*

unless of course
to front the sheen
of coming home

*

or rising
to the turn
of verses
at the slippery edge
of a hand

*

all that intolerable information
before you
feeling your way
at the wheel
despite the sorry music

*

half-shut
shut windy sky
palm fronds tumbling
and more sky
and this at the end of the mind

*

dreamt I was dreaming
and woke in sleep
going unusually fast
on the slipperiest of breezes
where it meets Beverly

*

fingering a stop
notebook's edge
pen tip
here there

*

an utterance
not its image
or impression
this the divide
it seems
and device

*

roof roof
says the blind pup
stymied otherwise
by angels pronouns
and more unwilling
accomplices

*

between a bump
and another
deliberately dark
two step
one-two
two step

*

and above what
shadowing sounds
might the sound
of your hello

*

among the grace now
of one or two honks
in far salmon sky

MOTIVE & OPPORTUNITY

"Language is never innocent."
—Roland Barthes, *Writing Degree Zero*

"It's a bright and guilty world."
—Orson Welles, *Lady from Shangai*

SCENE OF THE CRIME

Hallway lights likely burned out
and the faintest whiff of ocean
coming this way. You stop in a doorway,
cheek on cold plaster, and wait.
You sense the story has no ending,
the heart shadows whom it will,
turning right or left in the gloom.
And what's probably about to happen
is it part of the intrigue or
just the kind of coincidence
you've learned to distrust? There,
something dragging, and a warmish
sensation before that tang of salt air.

SATURDAY MORNING

You try the doorknob again,
a few minutes after six
the first Saturday in March.
You force yourself to breathe
nudging open the door.
How easily will you find it?

You step into the wide kitchen
off the porch, light unfolding
over treetops along the hill.
You begin to feel almost at home,
like turning on the radio,
putting on coffee and going back out
to fetch the paper from the driveway.

Who knows? shifting your eyes
to the empty sink, row of cupboards,
glint of a glass door next to the fridge.
You're breathing a little easier now
almost certain that you're alone.

1469 AMALFI DRIVE

Even if you can't recall how it happened
more than half a century ago.
Probably she said something to you
and took that easy step. One morning
most likely after serving mass,
at once you were behind the rectory,
on the landing under the stairs:
full, pale lips, that pert, budding chest.

The memory only a week ago
as you headed west on Sunset,
light traffic that brought you early
to 1469 Amalfi Drive.
And then it happened as scripted.
Husband and wife, both ready for you.

JEOPARDY

The crime always feels like yours.
That you'll gamble happiness,
your own and everyone else's,
just to understand, to uncover
some mysterious combination
of thoughts, images, commonplaces,
adding up, you hope, to nothing less
than a confession. As for motive,
one might as well question the point of
dereliction, or evil itself.

LATE

Did you say that you've been here before
and that somehow eases the shock,
the tawdriness of what you discover,
nudging open the door with your elbow,
following the traces of blood out back
into the well-kept yard of roses,
avocado and lemon trees?

Does it get easier, maybe familiar,
that final gesture, the position of the hands
in relation to the rest of the body?
And that question you hardly ever bring up
or almost never consider pursuing?

As you step around the rickety gate
at the side of the house, you wonder
what you expected to find, how late it is,
how bad the traffic on your way downtown?

DOWNSTREAM

And with that giddy, long-awaited
sensation of being adrift and
slipping downstream toward a pale horizon
at last the words come.

So much lighter, even extravagant,
and at once more measured than expected.
A declaration rather than a confession,
something lingering hidden from sight.

To close the eyes and let the oars
slip from the fingers. To close your eyes
and remember the name, the name swirling
ahead of that abiding glimpse downriver.

NEIGHBORS

It isn't that you see any of this
heading toward a conclusion. More of
a notion, maybe some uneasiness
about what's coming with neighbors like these.
Not to speculate or look ahead,
but considering the case is dragging
and so much still to be established.
The nature of the crime, for instance,
as in your mind it barely has a name.

Too soon to worry about limiting
the investigation. Pulling over
in front of the rambling property,
you can't help being charmed by the shades
of bougainvillea – purple, yellow, red
and white – that balance the dazzling air
and ocean views in a setting like this.

EVIDENCE

Now you're right in the middle, sleepless nights,
a summer cold coming on and little to show for it.
A double homicide downtown at rush hour
with a handful of witnesses who didn't see a thing.

No murder weapon, of course, and those first
on the scene didn't do a very good job
except at pointing fingers. Can't even think
of starting over with little more than
a jumble of rumors and contradictions.

It's a wonder you keep at it. *It*, vaguer by the day,
and a crime that seems, like everything else,
just to fade away. No past, no present,
but a glum, sprawling future that has us all pretending.

TURNING OVER

And the sleepless nights
paddling around heartache,
and rain barely audible,
flipping pages, whispering
of cool sheets, and hope
that day finally comes,
scribbling in a notebook
until turning over
on your back. And a long
deliberate breath before
bobbing out on the falling tide.

A KEY

Last time you meet your old friend hands you
an envelope with a key to his back door
in case, as he says, something happens.
You've flown into town for his birthday,
just the two of you and his girlfriend.
You all look very happy, considering.

You can't talk enough about the empty
store fronts, no decent cafes, the corny place
your hometown has become. Next morning you meet
on your way to the airport, shake hands at the corner
of the building where you were born, your old friend
reminding you to keep that key in a safe place.

A NAME

You're left alone on a bed in a room.
They circle you, showing their fists,
the knobby fingers and smiles.
You tell them you're hopeful, you say,
hopeful. They laugh, faces twisted
with rage at your cautious voice.

You tell them that you've been sick
and don't care, and they grin
even more, moving closer.
They keep the lights off and
you try to wake up screaming.
They show fingers, knuckles,
open fists, even closer.

A blond one finally speaks
what they say is your name,
and you try to stand still,
sit down, to stop your fingers
and hands twitching. Only the
unshaven rabid smiles now
familiar in the dark circling
evidence of arms and legs.

A WALL

Swallows and mulberries, and a wall
at start of day. Exotic, you suppose,
as morning seeps through the curtains.
That morning. Any morning. A hell of a
way to begin. Or at least go on.

They're letting you out today, mostly
in one piece. A kind of happy man
with a joy between your teeth that would kill
most people.

        The trouble with absolutes,
one wants to say, until you call up
those old words, hateful, ignorant, stupid
words one never forgets. A murky wall,
a little unreal even from the start.

INNOCENCE

Stale summer seeping through the blinds,
on the table tumblers of melted ice,
a pack of Chesterfields
and you trying not to yawn.
Does she keep that vague smile
when you hear steps on the stairs
and pretend to reach for your
cigarettes to see behind her?
Before the knob begins to turn
and the door fly silently open?

Aren't you now playing it over:
delicate fingers, her silly almost
innocent grin, your weight shifting
from the chair, reaching for your ankle
and cold steel that's your only salvation?
Why can't you remember what she's
about to say, if anything at all?

A PICTURE

Of course it's always been a town where
no one asks questions. And you were here first,
even if those times don't mean so much now.

The contradictions keep piling up,
the days getting longer and hotter.
So who was it coming up the stairs,
who left traces of pale lipstick, a hint
of lavender on the pillowcase?

How much does her picture really mean?
What can you read in a look, or events
that harmonize, appear and disappear?
Who still believes in accidents
when everyone has the same alibi
and denies the reason they're even here?

CLOUDS

They hang heavy to the northeast
unmoving in the sultry light.
You pull into a gas station, fill up
and buy a coke. Cold plastic in your hand
you think of all the times you've stopped to think
like this, a sinking sun, night air static
with neon and brash impossibility.

You pull out south on Glendale, too early
to call in, nothing on your phone,
too many coffees to give it even a
second thought. Traffic's light enough as
you poke at the screen and learn the chances
of evening showers downgraded again.

PANAMA

for Susanna Rabitti

You have an extra cup of coffee
and a long shower. Couldn't say where
the whole thing's leading though now you're
pretty sure who isn't the murderer.

Put on your favorite tie for the drive downtown,
a bubbly blue thing you got from your daughter
last Christmas. Even showing up early
you'll have to listen to a load of crap like,
"Heard you're back from a few weeks in Paris,"
or "Glad to see you, we thought you'd retired."

And then you'll grin and lift your panama
in salute and look for an empty chair.

LONG STREETS

The latest break in the case just didn't pan out.
Sketchy evidence and a last-minute alibi
(fed-up wife of a to-remain-nameless politician)
ruled out our suspect, another city hall hot shot
it would've been o so sweet to nail. Leave nothing
to chance, go through the notes one more time.
Leave nothing out of the whole wacky scenario.
The players are all there, plenty of opportunity.

Maybe skip dinner, buy a sandwich and a beer
and drive up to the observatory. Looking southwest
across the city, mapping left to right the three longest
streets in the world. Figueroa, Vermont, Western,
endings hazy out there in the evening sun.
Maybe something will come as you eat your sandwich,
take a sip of beer, considering how much of
your life in this lost city begins to make any sense.

SO WHAT

More than a year since you've gone to a movie.
You prefer being home in your easy chair
with a book, sensing the night overspread
the garden, every time familiar
and always a little different.

It's a new release, a remake of an
80s classic, itself an adaptation
of a sci-fi standard set in L.A.
The protagonist is younger, prettier
than in the original. Everyone's cool
and athletic, with about as much appeal
as a bag of potato chips. The plot's glib,
all happening so fast with dazzling effects,
while nothing makes much sense until the last
ten minutes and by then it's too late to care.

Driving back home, top down, happy to
have a huge yellow moon over the hill
and the opening of Miles' "So What"
on the radio – ensemble's building
motive and then the three solos, bang bang bang,
Miles, Coltrane and Cannonball – night air
all over you as you're just about home.

HALL OF RECORDS

So who's the father? Punctuating
a taxi pulling out of a space
almost in front of the Hall of Records.
It's a drizzly Wednesday in March
near closing. After too long a lunch
at your favorite fish place in Pasadena,
you decide on a title search of some
courtyard apartments at a last-known address.

You're scribbling the half-slip of paper
when a neat little blond on the wrong side
of forty shows you her baby blues asking
if she might be of help. Back in minutes,
carrying a short coat and floppy hat,
she places the print-out on the counter.
You thank her and ask, "Do you like the rain?"
"Of course," she says. "And drinking?" you say.
"Certainly more interesting than singing."

You barely have to wait five minutes
when she pulls up alongside in a
green Chevy pickup flashing a smile.
Less than a couple miles down a tree-lined street,
she disappears into a driveway only
to reappear at the door of a duplex
without even a glance in your direction.
You finish your cigarette and ring the bell.
The neat little blond opens the door
and just about bowing, welcomes you in.

VALENTINE

So who then was the father and why
the grandmother and the rest begins
to fall into place. Her property
is only one street over on Valentine,
and through the garages, down a driveway,
you're there with no one really noticing.

Can't find your pen. Must have left it in the car.
You cover the half-block in a sentence,
fish pen and notebook out of your bag
and back to the table, all the while
running down how it must have happened.

The story follows almost as expected.
Of course the alibis will take time to break
but these days you've got nothing but.
Once it's pretty much down on paper, time
to consider something stronger than coffee.

PORTRAIT

A mug's game, old Rosen used to grumble,
flicking ash into his coffee cup.
Most likely true seen from far enough away
though it brings little satisfaction
to scenes like this. When you first walk in
they're all around the grandmother's body that
looks about to say something from the corner
of a long sofa. "Your turn to write it up,"
says the Captain. "Take your time. Don't need it
back until the day after tomorrow."

A shot through the heart from the smaller sofa
where he'd probably sat hundreds of times
chatting with his guardian angel who loved him
most in the world. Then to the library,
the grandfather's, off the rear garden.
He'd taken his bourbon and soda
and sat in front of the old man's portrait.
Held a mouthful and pistol between his teeth
and fired. Top of his head all over the painting.

Have much of what you're going to need.
Mother gone for over twenty-five years,
leaving him and his sister in that big house.
Eventually turns up in Paris writing,
though apparently mostly in French.
The report's basically preliminary
but how to begin: *In a fit of blind rage*….
Sure, it will take time to tie up loose ends
and someone like you who reads enough French.

NUMBER

In this business there's always another day.
And another. The case winding down,
tomorrow's a lazy afternoon of reading
or napping or a long walk along the river.

A life like any other, an Irish friend
liked to say, expert in afternoons.
Once in a great while, time slows to a crawl,
like summers in high school – no clue who you are,
only the awful sense that it might ever
be this way. Think it through, get it all down
and cross out much of what you've written.

Over the years you've learned to listen
but it helps only so much. Nothing's changed.
The stakes remain pitifully small, remote
by any reckoning. You get up to have
some water, a cup of coffee, wondering
where you managed to put the woman's number,
why wasn't it there in your notebook last night?

9 781848 617155